Dropshipping Ecommerce in 2019

By

Chris McDonald

Table of contents

Chapter 1: Understand How Dropshipping Works.... 1

    Introduction To Processes And Works of Dropshipping 1

Chapter 2: The Advantages of Working in Dropshipping 6

    Limited Investments To Start 6

    Easy To Get Started 8

    Lots Of Products To Choose From 9

    It's a Business That You Can Do in a Global Market 11

    Easy To Scale Up 14

    Easy To Automate 17

Chapter 3: The Issues of Dropshipping 21

    Sudden Shortages In Stock 21

    Potential Issues With Quality Control 22

    Supplier Errors & Hard To Find Products That Will Make Enough Money 24

Chapter 4: How to Start With a Dropshipping Business 29

    Choose The Right Niche 29

    Find A Market Supplier 32

Get Your Sales Tax ID 36

Pick Out Your Products 41

Choose Your Selling Platform 45

Setting Up Strategy to Bring Customer In 51

Pick The Right Price 54

Chapter 5: How to Pick a Supplier and How to Pick Out the Product 55

How to Pick a Good Supplier 55

How to Pick Out the Right Products to Sell 58

The Steps to Take For Choosing the Right Products 61

Chapter 6: Handle Customers with Excellent Customer Service 68

Understand your customers 68

The Steps On How to Give Excellent Customer Service 71

The Fulfilment of the Customers Is The First Priority 83

How to Differentiate You From the Competitions 86

Chapter 7: How to Handle Security Issues with Business Strategy 90

Select A Platform that is Secure 90

Set Higher Standards For Passwords 92

Protection Against Any DDoS Attacks 93

Allocating bandwidth 95

Call Your ISP or Hosting Provider 97

Creating the DDoS Playbook 100

Get In Touch With a DDoS Mitigation Expert.... 103

Use an SSL Protection Layer 105

Chapter 8: How to Scale-Up Your Business 109

Add More Products to Your Inventory and Consider Seasonal Items 109

Hire Others Collaborators to Help You Manage The Business 113

Chapter 9: How to Dropship with Shopify............. 117

Chapter 10: How to Dropship on Amazon and eBay 120

Dropshipping On Amazon 120

Dropshipping on eBay....................................... 123

Chapter 11: Creating a Personal Website for Your Dropshipping Business... 124

Get Your Domain Name And Web Hosting 124

Install WordPress 125

Set Up the Website And Pick The Right Plugins 125

Chapter 12: Social Media Approach in Dropshipping 127

Social Media Marketing approach 127

 Facebook Ads 131

 Google Adwords 136

Chapter 13: How Amazon FBA Can Help You Grow Your Business 139

 Approach to Amazon FBA system 139

Chapter 14: How to Dropship in the Practical Way and How to Sell Effectively Your Products 143

 Open the Horizon 143

 Indirect Marketing 151

 Product Management 152

 Consistency 154

Chapter 15: Tips to Make Your Dropshipping Business as Successful as Possible 156

 Focus On the Marketing 156

 Do Not Underprice the Products 158

 Pick a Product That Makes a Good Profit Margin 161

 Find Ways to Bundle Items Together 163

 Pick the Right Platform 165

 Always Provide The Best Customer Service 166

 Verify Your Products Personally Before Selling It 167

Conclusion 171

Chapter 1: Understand How Dropshipping Works

Introduction To Processes And Works of Dropshipping

We are in a new world of commerce and welcome! Have you been here before? If you have not we can just jump right in and talk business. Unlike the traditional means of supplying customers with products by exchange or other business or processing services, there is a rising trend in the promotion to regular retail commerce to online e-commerce which can be done from anywhere in the world. Dropshipping is helping to automate our e-commerce markets around different countries that may also have different means of exchange and with these different levels, there will also be new tariffs and taxes.

Allowing E-commerce throughout new territories is highly profitable for valued goods that are new, refurbished and even unseen goods. With a dropshipping system, there will be new relationships made to further the business dream. Considering that you will want a new system it will come with a price but with a strong business and relatable mission model, there will be profits made back in no time and become one of the leading shops. The struggles that most businesses run into are the learning parts that must take place to run a proper e-commerce store with increasing gains.

With Dropshipping businesses are choosing to distribute through the help of other companies that can feasibly handle the work and satisfy the needs of the business owners. Corporations make decisions to deal exclusively with whoever they like instead of a broad circuit and their relationship ties can benefit in this diversity. This can also create a unique selling market specifically for the business. Dropshipping minimizes on many costs and some of them include product quantity. When it comes to shipping and handling there are many ways you can go about your services but you also want to do the most cost-efficient strategy for your business budget.

Dropshipping helps with product diversity and assures the seller to have a secured product line that gets significant motivation from their buyer. This minimizes on assets the business could be giving into the business and allows room for the comfortability of net flow. The business can dedicate their energy to another system and in this process also increase capital. With a new outlook, the business owner can create freedom and even the capability to work from home managing the owner's e-commerce shopping store. The business owner can choose any product of their desire. The profit will expand a business into a new organization that can become bigger than it.

There have even been a few non-profit organizations that have profited for charities using Dropshipping free products under the proper business model. There are a ton of ways dropshipping is going to alleviate a lot of time and possible stress on the agenda for the e-commerce online shop. If the business owner has tasks in the daily life that are not in line with the e-commerce business it will be important to balance all of the work tasks at hand.

The business will be using the positive motivation of the product or products in the current inventory and trustworthy roles for delivery to speak of the overall goal of the company and mission standpoint. These two elements are crucial for buyers across the global market to order and pay for products of exchange and even electronic services alike.

Millions of e-commerce websites have strived off of keeping these very simple steps in mind that you will learn about in this book. The business will maintain a structured revenue balance if they consider all of the steps in a Dropshipping journey for the e-commerce shop.

Chapter 2: The Advantages of Working in Dropshipping

Limited Investments To Start

One of the best qualities of beginning an online store presence with Dropshipping capabilities is that there doesn't need to be a huge investment to begin. As long as the fees and enrollments are tended to the whole system can be a rather low budget costing. One must create a simple budget that is feasible in their situation and become more aware of the earning potential. The truth is that the less investment you put in at the beginning the less profit that you will get back in the long run or over time. This is not always the case if you can play good in the game of e-commerce. When the business first makes their step into e-commerce they also need to know their limits of investments.

It's important to get the basic steps in first before you jump all in with all of your money on one product shipment or filling the inventory to have every piece because we have to remember that the buyers are going to be an important part as well. We will get onto that point later in the next chapters but understanding your limits is a good start to have.

Remember that there is competition around every corner so consider the fact that there are other businesses like yours that may be in the same profit regime. We do not want to set the limits too low that they will not sustain the business model or standards set out. Just because there can be a lost cost of entry the truth is that you may need to invest more than the bare minimum to begin making the profit e-commerce will bring. Do not be intimidated by the competition that will be alongside your product line because there is room for everyone in this e-commerce world.

Easy To Get Started

This is going to be a small financial risk that you have to take and have to gear up for which moves we are going to make to see revenue come to our business. There have to be urgent actions done for the great experience of the customers. Information and product descriptions are going to be the next second habit that you develop so that you can also ensure that you are a master of your craft. If you don't know everything about the product line that's okay, but we recommend that you have some extended background knowledge about the products in your inventory just in case you run into a problem with a customer that needs extended information on the product that you sold and shipped them.

Lots Of Products To Choose From

You may be considering the products plentiful to you and maybe adding more and more to your inventory as we speak. Do not stack this tower too high or things will topple and your inventory can come crashing down. Don't be caught off guard with too much to hold and a crashing halt. When the company adds too much inventory to their business catalog, there can be a difficult time moving inventory out of the warehouse and this can become problematic.

Some inventory may not be selling at all, and there may be other problems with popularity or bad review of products you have in your inventory. There can be inventory that you have that individuals have purchased and left bad reviews about on other e-commerce websites. This is a business that you can do in a global market and that means that you are going to expand your market through countries and cities everywhere. Do not judge any avenue that you try to market towards and reach out to every potential prospect that you possibly can find and define a better demographic of buyers.

You are going to find customers that are looking for a steady supply of the product line you have and there are going to be one–time buyers that will help your profit. Every customer must be treated the same with importance and respect to ensure that everyone knows that you are a reputable establishment. One of the basic things you are going to need at all times is WiFi and you will be able to track your online business anywhere you are at using a self-made calendar and an optimized application made for your money services. This will create an urgent mindset for the business because some order will come in and they will need to be handled with some time sensitivity.

Be aware that you will be supplying customers with products that they may rely on for their business. This is why it is important to follow these simple steps to create a useful presence on the internet. The business has to be profitable in every way for there to be an enjoyable workflow. Follow your instincts with product choice and get ready to begin. You are just going to get geared up for a few extra steps you must take you may not have heard of before. This is where we are going to be thankful we don't own a whole warehouse we have to both staff and management. We are skipping the middleman and we are going to become the go-to for our shop's great experience.

It's a Business That You Can Do in a Global Market

Global e-commerce is going to be a new world and you are going to find that you are not alone here. There are going to be striving companies just like yours that need the same amount of attention and passion to achieve the success it entails. Just because there are other dropshippers out there with you on the web that doesn't mean there needs to be competition between two corporations. No business should ever have to compete with a business like Amazon because there is room for everyone and there is the same general focus shared.

Since it is a global market you are going to be taking orders and making shipments at different times and different places. You can practically make sales overnight and have your product in full rotation by the time you wake up to have coffee the next morning. There aren't going to be an open and closing signs for your shop because it's going to have a 24/7 presence online and this is going to maximize all opportunities for profit. Recognize that you may need to even do some interpreting because customers will come from every walk of life to just have one of the products on your line today.

We just need to figure out the best way we are going to market to our global crowd and how we are going to create a likable and shareable space for everyone coming to visit. Use simplicity when choosing your marketing points for your new global crowd. Our buyers must share the same interests and find the same importance in the business that is online. There must be deep connections and feelings attached to the store, and this is going to increase reputation value in more than just the community downtown. It is important to reach out to the customers that will build our foundation because they will spread our name to their close ones and corporations.

When we can establish a connecting and trustworthy space for your customers it's going to bring their close ones as well to the sites you set and this will create a greater fan base for your products. Once there is a strong structure of customer traffic you will begin to receive reviews to your store and the products inside and this is going to connect even more customers in the world. Others will be able to see new reviews that your faithful customers are kindly leaving and this is going to attract new crowds to purchase the other inventory they are unaware of.

This is going to be a new load of work since you are marketing everywhere around the world, but you are going to see a return come to your business because this isn't going to be a normal community reach. The global market you create may solve problems that customers have had for years as long as you can be a trustworthy source of supply and you will be the only shop that they choose to go to.

Easy To Scale Up
You may not be able to afford everything that you are going to learn about if you are starting

with a low budget. But this is why we are going to ramp up production simply by just beginning. You will find more and more forward motivation with the decision you decide to make and that includes every shipment. Once you are making consistent sales every week and you notice that orders are coming in annually you may want to consider scaling up your productions. Truth is that you most likely are not going to see sales immediately come in the first day and especially if you have done no extra marketing for your site.

Give it some time and you are going to see a great return. If you have a high end and popular item in your e-commerce inventory, then we can consider the fact that you may need to get ready for the number of customers you are going to have right from the start to your site. Do not be afraid to use all means of advertising which can include user applications and social media to your advantage. Remember that you are going to scale up your store's traffic and that is going to mean finding a specific buyer crowd that has targeted interests. Look into blogs and forums that have other individuals asking frequent questions and give them helpful links to your store and see where it will get the business.

You are going to be an e-commerce shop that supplies the everyday individual and they couldn't need just a few units, but maybe a hundred units from your store. We are going to need to ramp up inventory capacity and find new ways to keep up with the demand of the customers that trust the businesses services. You may be selling a hundred or two hundred units a day and this will be because they are not high value enough to see a high return on. This will make your profits come in slower, but you will still profit nonetheless and we have to remember how much work this would be for one person every day if there were no warehouse with employees to make magic happen. Moving hundreds of units every day is going to take work and we have to be honest about this.

Easy To Automate

There are customers in other cities that will need your products on time advanced schedules and you can automate recurring shipments and this can give you so much time to do your other Dropshipping duties. Remember that there are tools that can do exactly what you have been asking for. We have to consider all of the ways that automating your services with other services is going to create a stable structure for learning about perfecting this craft.

Create templates that export sales orders using dropshipping systems. The inserted templates will then auto-populate when an order is received on whatever marketplaces or shop checkouts that the business deal with. It'll then be forwarded to your supplier as an email with a

CSV attachment and this is going to act as an internal invoice. There will be agreements and surely; even a negotiated contractual agreements that assure the services provided will be fulfilled as well. Shortly after the order will be fulfilled, and all information that is about the product and package will be sent to the buyer for confirmation. This process can be done while the business owner is tending to other tasks unrelated without even having to opening an app or check in and out of tedious tasks.

VA's are a good way to go for a good way to manage your order fulfillment, and all you have to do is be one or you can hire one. Marketing agencies can handle your advertising presence online or in person, and there can even be a possible web developer hired and as well some electronic customer support system that you know the customers will be happy with in case running into any problem. Remember that you are going to be handling a lot in the beginning phases of the e-commerce shop so it may not be the easiest thing to dive completely into automated Dropshipping.

It is recommended that the business owner can get used to handling and shipping the products using every trial and error so that the process is all acquainted. We need to also understand that it's not necessary to automate your dropshipping system early so that you are trying to move out the entire inventory you have out the door in complete stress. The most cost efficient tactic the business can take for their online automation is critical, but we must make sure are all aware of the exact duties we must fulfill to run a successful online shop.

It is best to do the most you can with your e-commerce business on your own. You are going to learn a lot of dos and don'ts of your business and have full control of your business. There must be full control of the business so that you are not on the sidelines and unaware of any random occurrences. A dedicated owner is going to be at the front lines of their business and the customers are going to see it with trust. Your profit will be higher with a promise to expand even further with your global presence. Of course, this all only applies if you are in a growth/startup phase and you are at least somewhat able to do these tasks on your own.

Remember that you are going to be spending money on these services to automate the dropshipping done for your e-commerce store. Nothing is free, but there are some pretty decent rates as long as you find all of your options online before you make that choice with your trusted company. You are going to be spending money to do your business and it may seem like money is coming and in without balance, but it's your job to truly make sure that you are receiving pure profit if not breaking even to meet your monthly income plan.

Chapter 3: The Issues of Dropshipping

Sudden Shortages In Stock

Inventory management is going to become the main factor in handling a dropshipping website because inventory is going to change every day with every shipment being set and your products purchased. Inventory is going to need to be kept track of every day and thankfully you can also automate this service. Connect your suppliers and monitor their inventory levels with an application and other means to track monthly profits. If they sell out of the product in the warehouse inventory, your store will automatically list the product as unavailable on any marketplaces. Remember that we can be saving some valuable time and we can pay attention to product trending to find our specific buyer crowd.

There is a real possibility that you will have less control over your own business through the process of automation. Some businesses have to get used to this type of change in their monthly planning and processes. Considering that you are going to let a system handle most of your processes is worthy of the trust card. Businesses need to make sure they are associating with other proper businesses that perform with professionalism and time-critical responses. Do not fear this new world of assistance because it is going to aid you in achieving more profits for the fiscal month. Just see where it will take you even though you have lost some control.

Potential Issues With Quality Control

Quality is going to be one of the main assets to keep in control when the company is sending out hundreds of units to their trusted buyers. A system that can handle the inspections of the products and reviews of the whole manifest will create more room to make sure the customer is getting the right product and that it's going through proper packing before it gets to them. Checking on the simple things are going to be the first thing the company will be striving for and these include proper packaging, labeling, and quantity. Labels need to be readable with a white background and contain sufficient product information. The label needs to be scan-able to RFID or other tracking codes and there should be no other misrepresenting information. The packaging needs to prevent water and other material from getting inside.

Considering that these some of these shipments are going overseas a carton drop test is necessary and it can simulate how the packages will do if they are handled roughly. Double checking the quantity of the inventory that is being shipped will be important as well for minimizing jack loads. This could make it easy for one individual to carry the inventory in rather than need a dolly or another tool to unload. It is cost effective to make sure that most of these needs are met by the manufacturers or distributors before it gets to the seller's consumers hands. Making that middle tie easier is going to help the workload of the seller being able to manage their inventory at a higher caliber.

Supplier Errors & Hard To Find Products That Will Make Enough Money

A problem that will arise in e-commerce is the reality of cancellations and returns on shipments. There will come a time where the business will see the package returned to sender and it will have to go right back to the warehouse. A pedigree dropshipping shop will not let this phase the company and they'll have to gather the next steps to satisfy every customer or returning customer that came to their shop. Fulfilling the orders of the customers that return products are going to leave a sweet and generous feeling inside of the customer that might lead them back around one day to shop again. Make sure there around clear directions and website guides on your returning process.

This will ensure that the customer has the most shop friendly experience going to a shop that they feel comfortable in. Make sure you do everything on the back end when you finally specify returning details and be a part of every process in case there is any kind of confusion or any novice buyers. This will create a good atmosphere for your shop and it will bring more buyers to come. We want to also make sure we can deliver a timely refund to the customers that return products. We want to deliver timely receipts as well and create a simple process for everyone involved.

Guide everything in the right order whether it means that you have the customer mail the product back to you while you after sending the product back to the supplier. You can also instruct the buyer to send the product back to the supplier but this is going to give you a delay in payments and refunds. Keep in mind that everything is on different time schedules and you want to keep the time of the customer of the highest importance.

One problem of dropshipping is the delay in orders pending delivery. It can even harm the future business of your customers. If other businesses rely on you to maintain a consistent package delivery route, then there needs to be secure knowing that your delivery and shipping regulations will be monitored. If there are any upcoming change in delivery notifications that you will need to relay your customer then make it the first priority to notify that the customer's shipment will be tardy.

It is so crucial to prioritize the suppliers that you welcome into your shop front to supply the business. We must pick good suppliers that stand behind the demand for the shops and one that will prioritize us back. The reputation of the e-commerce shop is only as good as the drop shipping partner. We have to create a professional atmosphere that supports our professional presence in the e-commerce shop.

Backorders can be a hassle if you do not deal with a supplier that has a good process on their handling. Cancel this item instead of letting it skip to back order and it will save you a lot of trouble. You do not want to deal with a supplier that also goes through a third party to get your product shipped. Avoid complicating your dropshipping equations with companies that make it hard or time-costly for you to get the products to your customers.

The more suppliers you use, the more items you're able to sell and we are going to need serious sales to have serious success dropshipping. The problem is that the more products you sell and the more suppliers you work with, the more difficult it becomes to manage it all by hand with the books. This is where automation needs to step in to help because as the business owner typically we are only one person and must not crush ourselves with the workload we accept.

Dropshippers typically work with multiple suppliers and this can be a strong advantage for you to have for your global market. Work with multiple suppliers and find the balance of product diversity that will separate you from other shops. Be ready for the workload working with multiple shops will bring because you'll see a great return for the amount of work you can put in for the businesses global reach.

Chapter 4: How to Start With a Dropshipping Business

Choose The Right Niche

The business is going to need to jump in the right niche that supports the full mission of the business. It must be something that the company owner is invested or interested in and they should be able to display these interests through the product shop and this will, in turn, bring more buyer traffic. Focus on the specific goal you have for the shop and the buyers alike so that there will be returning buyers that can share the same experience with someone else that you have given them through your e-commerce site.

There needs to be some type of passion for the dropshipping business you are going into because considering you are going to putting a lot of your time into it. You will not want to get burnt out on your product. If you feel like you are becoming discouraged about the products that are in your shop, you will lose energy for the direction you have been trying to go with your shop. Find your audience because you cannot just expect your audience to find you. Marketing is going to be one of the mainstays of having an e-commerce shop.

Since you don't have a physical storefront that buyers can see with their own eyes while they are driving on the street you are going to need to bring a presence right to them if it means electronically or putting flyers up all around town with your shop's name on it. Once you are creating a better scope for your fan base it is going to be necessary to see who your audience is. The business must see who is purchasing their products and what possible demographic do they fall in. Find an optimization tool for your business and track all data that is incoming and outgoing from the business.

Customers make conversions on your shop's site and this means that their clicks and even the amount of time spent on the website is tracked. This could tell you further details about what might intrigue your future buyer. The software will be able to show you a path of the customer's wandering until it finally got them to the shopping cart which has given you a new purchase in your inbox. This is going to create a friendlier customer experience when they come to your site now that you know the things you may also have to work on ensuring that the customer will leave and come back happy again.

Find A Market Supplier

Finding a market supplier isn't going to be an easy one and done. There is going to be some suppliers that you choose to work with at first but they may not intend to stay your supplier forever. It's okay to lose some suppliers along the way, but businesses must be aware of the pitfalls of some supplier's courses that can send the businesses shipments and products into that might not be fit for your customer demands. A good market supplier is going to be one hundred percent transparent with you and they are going to have a contractual agreement.

Every step must be agreed upon by both parties and there will be consistent help and guidance during any rough parts of the first dropshipping orders the business has with the company. Reimbursements will be made if the company fails to perform the duties promised to the dropshipping company and they should generally have the better idea of the business's customer in mind. There must be complete cooperation for the whole process to work and for the dropshipping business to make a comfortable place in their online presence.

Good suppliers with prioritizing every dropshipper they have so that they can also maintain a positive reputation to other routes that they will also make with future business. We must address to not feel personal about letting a supplier go as a business partner to partner it is okay to go a separate way and disconnect. Do not wait until it is too late to disengage from the sour relationship tainting your shipments because it is going to save the business money and time before it is wasted spent on making up for the supplier's faults.

Do not be willing to lose any revenue for a bad market supplier because they are only a second party for your business and they are going to generate revenue for nothing in return. This can be why e-commerce shops that deal with global markets are choosing to deal with more than one supplier and this can be beneficial to their inventory. Dropshipping opens doors to engage exclusively with only certain companies and if there is a conflict of interest it can all be avoided by choosing the right suppliers and service software to help along the way.

Business can fully customize how their shop is run from the ground up and this can ensure that the most money is being made from the shop site. There are great partners formed through this kind of company communication and there must be an open mind to new approaches for this to happen. Become engaged with greater communities that are also in the same line of product. Welcome other parties or establish meetings and/or conferences with other individuals that share these gains with you because they will also be able to tell you more from a supplier's perspective.

The better you get to know the supplier that you deal with daily the faster you will begin to make more efficient revenue for the greater of the business. Knowing every piece of the puzzle truly helps here because it paints a greater picture for the storefront to see how their product is moving from the shopping cart to the doorstep and how. It is going to open up new ways to also optimize the customer experience. Automation software can edit supplier availability and choose which supplier fulfills your company's product. If that supplier sells out of an item, the order will be automatically resent as a manifested document or form of through-action to the next supplier you've prioritized.

You can avoid overselling and any back ordering issues that are occurring in the shop. Choosing to automate the process of prioritizing suppliers makes Dropshipping with multiple suppliers a more user-friendly experience for the business owner. The business may not be able to only go to the one supplier for all of its needs so there needs to be optimization somewhere along the line. There must be every avenue covered and the business cannot expect just one supplier to help with unless you are just looking for that one perfect company that is going to fulfill every single need that the business has.

Get Your Sales Tax ID

To receive an EIN for a business is free and fairly simple. The IRS accepts applications for EINs in ways be means of fax, online, by letters in the mail and by calling the main office. The business EIN is very unique just as the social security number is unique for a single individual. Any operating business will be required by the IRS to obtain an EIN which is also referred to as the business tax ID number. You can provide this tax number now on documents for many different services and opportunities that are going to come for the business.

Trusts, estates and non-profit organizations can receive an EIN and some regulations can be used without even having employees working for the shop or not. This creates a whole new playing field for the businesses that may be employing individuals or businesses that own high assets they are looking to handle on their tax books to make a couple of personal tax cuts out of the personal accounts.

Apply for the business EIN and practically receive it immediately by going to the IRS website, or you can also complete it by fax, phone or mail. The business asks a few questions and the owner of the business will list if they are applying as a sole proprietorship, corporation, LLC, partnership or estate. The business is going to need to describe why they are applying for the

EIN. Typical reasons for filing this request usually are for starting a new business or for banking purposes.

You are going need to provide personal information and this is going to finalize some of the steps to getting the EIN. After the steps are complete and they are generating your new EIN the IRS will also send the document with your authentic EIN and you are going to save this document for future reference. When they send you the document it will be confirmed that the new EIN has been entered into the database and that the business can begin using it at the will of the company. Getting a state tax ID number will change the way the business does exchanges with other parties and how they will file their taxes at the end of every fiscal year.

Receiving eligibility for a state tax ID number directly correlates if the business must pay state taxes. Sometimes you can use state tax ID numbers for other functions like protecting against identity theft for sole proprietors. There are many ways that a state tax ID number will benefit not only the company but the individual as well and there can be further research done. Tax obligations differentiate on state and local level, so you'll need to check with your state's websites and find specific details on tax rates that can vary from county to county.

States that do tax income will determine figures based on the structure of the business and business assets. Seven states don't have an income tax, and two others only impose a tax on income from dividends. Taxes also vary by state on working compensation insurance. Calculating startup costs and choosing a business structure at the beginning is going to give the business owner a better scope of what to expect their earnings to be their first or fifth year in business. All of these statues and regulations must be foretold to the owner as they can greatly benefit from many of the details set in play.

No matter which option you choose, you'll need the same information, beginning with your business name and address. You'll also need the type of business, such as sole proprietor, corporation, non-profit agency, farmers' cooperative or trust. Identify the reason you need an EIN. If you have employees working for your business record the number to expect during the next year. It's necessary to list any merchandise, products or services you offer when applying for the EIN because this is going to list tax deductions that you can make and it will benefit the business in many ways.

You'll now need the EIN to report your earnings to the IRS so don't forget about it next tax season because this is going to be the ticket to every dime reported. Once the application process is finished, this EIN will be with the business owner forever. If the owner decided that they don't wish to use this number anymore the IRS will close the business account under the name of the beholder but the EIN can never be canceled. If the individual needs this number in the future they can reinstate it but it will never be reassigned.

Pick Out Your Products

Remember that just because you are going to open up an e-commerce global shop that you are not trying to completely change the world to make this end-all-be-all of shops. Remember, there is competition everywhere you turn and it's going to be important to hold a strong place in the marketplace you reside and don't do anything that's outside of the business territories. Don't risk any assets of the business to make a new leap into dark territories that can harm the business like making new business agreements that can sign assets away or release partial ownership or stocks to third parties that are going to change the product line you set out.

It's important for the product line because this is what revolves around the general focus and mission point of any business. Do not try to change the game by selling products that are unheard of or are in truth unlikely to sell because this will confuse the market the business projects toward. Focus in on the crowd that you are interested in engaging in and follow trends to what they are interested in. This is going to bring more diversity to the shop and it will secure the product line. Create a constant flow of buyer traffic by similar products in your product line that relates to the products that are already flying out of the warehouse daily.

Once you hone in on the products that you know are going to sell you know that you have found your niche and that you can see constant revenue coming in to balance out the other services you maintain. There are affiliate programs that an individual can become part of just by selling products on their business sites. You may be selling something on your website right now that is possible to receive interest and affiliate pay for and this is something we recommend. This will also create a more solid foundation of the product line that is on the shop site because you will know that recurring traffic will come back to buy and buy again knowing that you represent popular products on your page that have the potential to sell out.

Find products that you know your customers are going to buy and make it relatable. Customers are going to come when they see something in the shop they may have seen in another shop with a high market value. The e-commerce business at play here could be offering that same item at a marked down price and this is going to be what brings in this new customer. The e-commerce site may just be the very first place the customer sees this product and this is why these choose out of product diversity to buy.

Trustworthy products from great suppliers are also going to keep a high buyer rate because this will mean that you represent a trusted product. Be constructive with your supplier if there is a need that you feel needs to be met and if you know the supplier can help you with a product-specific request then there needs to be one hundred percent cooperation on achieving the variations that can be made. Every change that you can make for the product line and shop itself is going to be going that extra mile for the customers that come to the shop.

Creating atmosphere is going to be important for the buyer because there isn't another way to tell a bad review from the buyer about how your site is doing and how it's treating them. You are going to need to optimize everything to the product line especially to create this type of environment for the buyer so they can buy and leave from the business page knowing exactly what they came for and exactly what the site represents satisfaction for.

Choose Your Selling Platform

There are going to be plenty of selling platforms to choose to do business with and picking one that can handle the workload is very important. The business will have to pick a proper platform to match their online presence. Before the business goes into purchasing the first, it is going to be necessary to track down all possible candidates and to calculate the costs of every single option on the web. The platform will have an attached fee to every service and this is necessary to ensure that every service performed is right for business.

If you already have revenue flowing into the business then you can justify jumping into a new selling platform but these fees can be costly if there is not a proper budget set in motion for a business in the beginning phases. Do not play catch up just trying to pay the fees as a new business because you will need to dedicate time and energy to the current objectives.

The platform the business will choose is one thing that should not be a cheap optional. It'll become an important investment for the business and even though that this step can come with expensive fees it must be noted that it's for a good reason to have the best for the business's sake. The platform will be standing with the business on the front lines and bringing a great experience to the next new customer that comes to visit the e-commerce shop.

Some platforms are going to charge you by different processing rates and these should be made aware of. All of the options for platformers are going to be paying a flat monthly rate which will correlate higher fees to transactions, bandwidth, server storage, and other application and application accessories. Every fee will need to fit with the business model to have a proper and organized budget structure. This is going to become an important decision especially when production ramps up and you are starting to see a new coming of different buying groups.

A great business is going to need a lot of powerful servers and bandwidth to use for all its customers. Web hosting is going to become another important necessity the business will undergo because you are going to be selling to customers all around the world. The business will also bring in countless numbers of traffic that will use a lot of data and need a lot of room for data to be stored as well. Poor web hosting for good platforms can downgrade the businesses search rankings and cause site loading times to be slowed; even causing sites to shut down bringing downtime to the buyer and owner.

There may be another host that is taking up more bandwidth around and that the current data provider is not able to perform under these conditions. We must make sure that all of the companies the business is going to trust will share the same common goals and that there will be no contingency. There must not be any interruptions from provider to provider and it is important that no lines are crossed within companies. For any service provider, the business will go through it will be a smart decision to always make sure they have 27 hours 7-day weeks support.

This is going to be vital to the livelihood of the e-commerce shop having to deal with late returns, misinformation gathering or general help about the products that are on the shelf for the customer that has questions to ask the distributor. If the hosting site crashes the business is also going to go down and in most cases, there will need to be a web developer's help to gain proper control again.

It's so important for that all-day contact access because if the site goes down we can surely say that the business will lose money every second that the site is down. Imagine that the day the site crashed was on a major holiday that everyone on the block is maximizing their sales on. This is not the day to lose these sales all from a cheap web hosting partner that cannot promise you the workload efficient for your site.

The business will need a strong manager to run the account once you choose the platform that is ready for the business requirements. It may do everything that you need it to do and the rest is up to whether it is user-friendly or not. A good software interface is necessary to create a comfortable experience for the business owner. The business will not want any technical problems associated with accounts linked to the dropshipping business. This is going to create inefficiency and possible customer confusion and anger.

The business needs to maintain a high priority of this user experience because the customer is going to expect a pedigree experience when it comes to handling their money and shipping information. Hire an adequate manager that is very experienced with electronic processing and things should go well from there. It's just important to understand that the platform must have standards to uphold for your company and by all means. The dropshipping business should deliver nothing but the best service for every customer that's in their order list.

Setting Up Strategy to Bring Customer In

Whether you are going to appeal to your buying audience by creating great rates for your products or creating a friendly user experience to drive high-end customers to high-end make purchases there must be a strategy in place. The business needs to have a customized strategy with the service providers that they choose to work with to all contribute to the same goal to achieve maximum profit all the way around. Appealing to your audience may not always be easy if you are in the beginning phases of the business but eventually, the owner will have to hunker down.

Creating a consistent flow to their e-commerce site is going to ensure that they make their quarterly goals and that they can keep the services for their dropshipping success in rotation. Strategies should be outgoing even if it involves adding all current customers to a newsletter that can affect their earnings on the next year they choose to spend money on the site. These strategies for marketing should reach out to the buyers current and new to engage them into opportunities on the site that may not have been there when they first joined. Lead new site visitors to feel welcomed looking at a certain section of the hosted page and create a feeling of joy and relationship as they scroll down the business product line.

Create interactive marketing strategies that bring in more customers and this could include flash sales where the prices on the product line are modified for a short amount of time to increase sales at a specific time. Create opportunities for your buyers to receive a shopping card for loyalty reward points that can be redeemed upon other purchases. Give incentives to your audience to buy and to also consider buying gifts for others if it is the gift-giving season.

Even these few examples will give the business site an edge for new and current customers alike to keep coming back to the site to see something new and special. This is going to set the business apart from other Dropshipping sites that may want to also increase their sales points for the quarter, but having our strategy in line before things come. it's going to make sure the customers visit us and not them.

A welcoming and engaging e-commerce site will allow the customer to feel free to optimize their wants in the business site. The more freedom that the customer has the more likely they will be willing to spend more money on a site. With these incentives in place, the buyer will become more and more attached to the company and they will begin to feel that the business is personalized for them and that it's going to be a trusted source to hopefully all of their needs.

Pick The Right Price

There is going to be a price zone that is right for the customer and the distributor. Pick a defined price that is going to be good for customers alike everywhere in the globe. You are going to be buying individually or buying in bulk and that is going to determine most of the price point. Develop this point so that you can make ends meet and pocket the profits that are going to come with every product that flies out. There needs to be a clever middle point met to welcome every class of customer that is going to come to spend money on your products. There need to be options for everyone if you are selling commodities, but if they are luxury items you are most likely going to have a high price point that competes with other luxury items for major profits.

Chapter 5: How to Pick a Supplier and How to Pick Out the Product

How to Pick a Good Supplier

When someone buys from you, you use that money to buy the product for less and have them ship it to your customer. That way there's little to no startup costs. Dropshipping can be profitable, but you need to know your niche inside and out. The products, the competition, the customer base, a clear value prop for your products, and a cost-effective mechanism to generate leads. So many people expect to source some cheap knock-off goods from China, set up a Shopify site, and start generating business immediately.

On the purchasing side, I'd recommend choosing your suppliers well. Preferably domestic, and preferably one that will let you submit POs electronically. This lets you automate your purchasing as sales increase, and reduces the risk that your sales contact will disappear (vacation, day of meetings, whatever) and leave your POs stranded for days.

The usual preference is wit in house fulfillment of a particular product as soon as it's proven with drop shipping and you can establish a pattern. Suppliers' markups on shipping usually leave a significant amount of assets on the table, and buying for a stock can build great rapport with the supplier.

Order from one source and see how their product management can hold up to the standard of your company. This will show the company what processes the company is partaking in and what shipping times and arrival dates will be true to attest. Shipping priorities are a major topic when it comes to timed orders and timed shipments. There could be a one or more day overdue gap that can send the Dropshipping company into straining to get their PO's filled in time.

All metrics of different retail selling systems must have a structured package manifesting system that works economically. Build a good system and structure with the companies chosen so that there can be a custom service provided. This will be the dropshipping system that's going to get practically hundreds of people their goods or resources. Having every order fulfilled on time is going to become an important factor.

It's often at times more important for the buyer than it's with the seller to get these goods promptly. These shops are what they rely on to perform services for others and in the end, obtain exponential profit through the company.

Designing a custom system that is going to feel comfortable and free to the buyers will allow them to nestle in and commit to a long term investment with the company.

How to Pick Out the Right Products to Sell

Picking the right product to sell is always a toss-up. The first thing to consider is that some products are trending right now and some products are on the other edge of the map. There may be a retro product that can make its way into the selling scene. How long is it going to be until they outsell and begin collecting dust again on the shelves after revamping for negative net gains? This is a revolving market typically in online global sales. The company needs to adjust its inventory with the hot and trending topics if they want to see their net gains skyrocket.

Adjust with the times of the day and age and see the sales increase monthly. There is always going to be changing trends and this is not a fear factor someone needs to consider. Investing more money into a personalized good product for the consumer is going to be worth going the extra mile. Some products are customized to say the customer's name or maybe a car that ha custom decals that were printed professionally.

Know the right product to sell to customers who are going to be coming from every corner of the world. The product needs to be a common good that is best found only at your source where the shop has its mission. Having product value and keeping an engaging inventory for the customer this is going to create a great customer experience that leaves them wanting to come back.

Sell something that you know just to see how important it is to be engaged. One must know the purpose of the product or have some type of knowledge of the product to make further profits from it. Research where to find the product because there may also be other sources and see what those sources are pricing those products for and price match if necessary.

If someone price matches you can sometimes advertise these facts as long as the company keeps up with the account information and price points. Sell things that you are surveying so that you know what the true worth is going to be and how you are going to optimize the market to make the most custom approach into the community. There are going to be companies who notice what you are doing and they are going to do on their end whatever they can to keep customers and also potential customers from being able to switch to your company.

The Steps to Take For Choosing the Right Products

1. Research A Product

It's the step where the seller is going to look at the product listings that are on all supplier sites. These listings could be for the same product and just under different classifications. These listings could include similar products but with different styles or variations and this is while the seller could be searching through multiple sources. When looking for a product the seller should know not to go completely wild with their choices because there has to be a common theme towards the customers coming to the shop.

There must be a relative piece of information or quality to the product so that all of the customers will relate and the business will see the most drive into their products when the customers proceed to pick up multiple items from your store. The business will begin to see what kind of products that customers will value and what ways the business is going to bring in more products like these to keep the audience engaged.

2. Create A Profit Goal and Calculate Costs and Fees

Create a profit and hold it at the top of your stats. This is going to be the goal that you go to when you look at the quarterly earnings. When the company creates this goal there other balances and budgets don't always go affected depending on how willing the company owner wants to play it safe. If you create a higher goal for expectation one of the true realities of that fact is that one will most likely have to start dishing out more money for their interests.

The higher the interest, the higher the value will be. This new goal there should be aware that the company will have to go through more work and seeing these better profits will be proof. Once this is organized the company must calculate the cost and fees of shipping, handling, and all other fees and services that the company will need to start shipping. These fees may include FBA fulfillment fees or money marketing fees that are tied to the account. These will be calculated for the monthly or yearly budget that the company will set.

3. Purchase A Product and List It to Dropship

Purchase the first product that the company is interested in selling. This product could be one of many but the company will not know until it begins selling out of the door and creating real revenue. Purchase the product that feels right putting back online keeping in mind that you are going to buy it possibly in bulk eventually and that you are trying to make a profit off of the first current amount. Purchase a product on sale potentially so that you can mark up the price on a different site and gain profit off of the baseline price that the distributors charge.

Next, the company is going to list their product online to any Dropshipping company that you are considering and this could be a company like Alibaba. List the product and name your price for individual units and bulks alike. This may be the first appearance that the company will be making as a dropshipper. This is one of the most crucial points to be breaking in new customer service skills in case a buyer does have an interaction with the seller. This will be a good learning step for anyone who needs to develop some of their representative skills and they will be moving the order on in no time and shipping their first product sold in no time, too.

4. Analyze Spending Data

Keep track of every penny spent and where it is going to. You are going to notice your net gains but this may not be the point where you cash out and begin spending on new items. This is not the time to load up on bulk again unless you know that you have made more than 40% of the profits back to hold into the investments. Keeping track of this data and spending at the right time is very important so that there are no backward movements and things that are lost.

Assets can be lost if there isn't stable foothold on the company budget. This is why we analyze spending and redirect it to places where it needs attention if the budget is derailing. The better moves the company can make for their production the easier the time the company will have made decisions like adding new inventory to the list or possibly hiring on someone on as an account manager. Ideally, all of it will just be to create a better spending focus and to maximize all of the earnings that the company will need to convert to keep this great process flowing.

5. Make Recurring Purchasing Adjustments

Begin to adjust the purchases the company is making. There are going to be certain products that the company will begin to notice may not be selling. These products might have other reviews on other sites that aren't favorable and this could be indirect advertising to your marketplace that's shedding a light that no one likes to see. Don't let another site's bad reviews define your products and altogether it may be better to just let those sites represent those products.

If the company is interested in spending more revenue to track down a better product that may have the same qualities then go with another company. If you can find a better price for a better and more quality item even if it looks different this is going to make gains. Distributors around the world see this seller's problem, so that's why there are many of them trying to make better items available for anyone wants to buy.

These suppliers are going to be very trustworthy if you find one that you can run with. Because these suppliers going to be part of the times and they are going to be product-aware for your company. This will essentially offer the creation of new trends with you and the supplier and this could maximize profits tenfold by being ten steps ahead of the market.

Chapter 6: Handle Customers with Excellent Customer Service

Understand your customers

The key to making customers happy is by understanding every single need or concern. The customer wants to feel valued when you tell the customer each step of a processor when you tell them they are an important part of the shop's livelihood. There are many ways you can make the customer feel good but the company must also understand the personalities of their customers. Designing a catalog that is going to suit your customers in every way is the first step to making a great impression on the global selling world.

You must know why your customers don't support certain brands and why they won't be making so and so purchases this year. Learn what makes the customer happy so you don't have to walk the minefield of trust. You can come out of the gate with a great product to sell and the customers will appreciate the fact that your company backs up quality. The better quality of the product line for the shop the more quality your customers will feel just by purchasing them from the shop site.

Some customers prefer to spend more money and this, in turn, makes them feel more valuable. Do not fear to keep that price at a high value if you know your customers feel willing to spend. This is going to create a trustworthy relationship for the customer to spend freely and give back to the shop that is bringing them the high-end items.

Understanding your customer is going to take you a long way through the market. There will be customers that you convert from other markets that become your buyers instead and if they were spending their money elsewhere they would come to your site and choose the better. Some customers might even leave reviews that may or may not include competitor pricing. This could give insight to many future customers that have not gotten to your shopping cart.

Every customer has their own needs and it's important to find out exactly what the consensus is so we can duplicate our processes and make every customer happy that's coming to the source to purchase again. Treat every customer with respect and encourage any other future customers to come in and take a look around.

There are referring programs just for having your customer involve their friends to shop at the site and with some type of incentive you will have your new shoppers with their carts in no time. Give referred shoppers an extra 10% off when they refer someone to visit your shop. This will increase the traffic of buyers coming in with their friends or loved ones now coming to visit the shop.

The Steps On How to Give Excellent Customer Service

1. Represent:

The first step going to represent the company to the customer. The company will make their first impression by showcasing the value of the product and not of the shop. At this point, the company will let the shop speak for itself as a true test to see if it suits the buyer and all of their needs. Make it clear the owner of the company that the customer is talking to someone is going to solve all their needs and welcome them in every way.

If the business owner is hiring a third party for the customer service requests than this needs to be a monitored system from time to time. There need update alerts that also go to a business owner inbox so that the owner can be well aware of every request that is being sent to the company. Each of these requests can have case ID numbers so that if there needs to be any history checking about past orders this can be done easily with an organization system dedicated to customer service.

2. Engage and relate:

Engage the customer and let them know that you are right there or within an hour or so the distance to reaching their concerns or complaints. Make it a point to communicate to the customers that if there are any questions they can be sent to examplerequest@exampleemail.com and they will be able to get back to the buyer in 24 hours or more. These are important things to consider when the customer may need to return one of the packages or to verify shipping details after the order is sent out for shipment. Relate to the customer when they are in need and a place of confusion.

At times the customer is not always going to know what the process entails for ordering new shipments and this is going to be the perfect time to create a helpful guide on how-to purchase with the shopping cart. This can be a great time to engage with the customer and be a teaching influence to the customer that may need to be walked through the process and relate to them that customers go through it all the time and that it is going to be a learning experience for everyone.

Next time they can come and shop alone without ever having to voice a concern because the company owner reached out and solved it on their own by creating an environment of freedom and helpfulness. Not all customers will be handled this way if there are an abundance of customers flowing in.

Will need to be a support system put in place so that every customer isn't forgotten about and that their problems are handled as they come in. There might be two to five orders that are posing a holdup and the company owner will need to systematically solve every one of them promptly. Those shipments get sent out on time and there are no wait times for anyone's packages.

3. Acknowledge:

Connecting with the customer and acknowledging their presence is one of the main ways to create long term buyers for the company site. The customer wants to be acknowledged at first by the company. They know they are noticed by the source and that their time is going to be valued and their feedback valued as well. Respond to all the feedback given your shop and all products inside as it will show appreciation to the customer and welcome back any time of behavior towards the shop.

Acknowledge all types of good behavior and if there is any violent or aggressive behavior towards the site put up an alert for blocking emails on the subscribed list. This is going to be necessary for creating a free and healthy environment for all buyers to shop on. Feedback is always welcomed. We need to make sure the buyers feel free to voice their product opinions and to leave good reviews so that the business can now compete with other online retailers.

Although competition may not be the business owner's first move for creating company growth it's going to be one of the first things on the customers' minds when they are considering buying products from multiple sources to weigh all values. There are many opportunities to bring customers in by price matching value that are on other shelves in other shops so that you can increase the clientele buying rate.

Some customers are going to be coming to your site because of better value or for higher quality and whatever the case is we need to acknowledge each and everyone needs our customer is coming for to ensure they leave the shop with a professional outlook on the company and its products. Do not shoot down requests by customers bluntly as they are most likely trying to give very critical feedback. Just thank the customer for their input and tell them how there are going to be changes made along the way to suit all customers for the greater of the shopping experience.

4. Reason:

There is going to be an occasional upset customer that may not have got what they expected to get or maybe there was a shipping mistake somewhere down the line. There are going to be customers with shipments that are time sensitive and their deadline might be coming up fairly quickly as they proceed to type you up to a message for an estimation on the package delivery date. This is the time the business owner is going to need to reason with the customer and assure every request they will have will be met with a strong answer.

Not every customer will be disgruntled and this is not something to fear with every customer. As a new owner, it is best not to panic over the answers that must be given to the customer. The answers could be anywhere from putting a stop on the shipment or requesting further billing information that will also put a wait on their package shipment. If there is an upset customer the business cannot deal with that type of behavior irrationally because it most likely will scare the customer away and leave them feeling offended from the site and its contributors.

Handle every customer with care and welcome the customer to feel like they can contact the shop for support at any time and that it will be at the most convenient that they will get a response to them promptly. Tell the buyer that their problem is understood and that it will be handled and solved. Never leave the customer feeling helpless or like their problem is so significant that it cannot be resolved. The customer will feel uncomfortable in this situation like they are at a loss and this could be bad for the results of the shopping cart.

The customer could also feel like they aren't making practical use of their time and that the site is taking more of their time more than they are gaining positive experience from the site. Right these wrongs if they occur because your customer is only a click away from never seeing them again. We need to create a healthy atmosphere to have a great experience on our site and going about their days knowing that they successfully ordered from our online shop.

Know About Your Products

Become a master of your craft even if this product is not something you are completely knowledgeable about. The owner must have great product insight and be engaged with the product to know where the company is going to go with a few weeks worth of work. If the company grows to new proportions it is going to bring new populations that are going to demand more products. The product diversity is going to bring on new customers and that with new products will bring new product management.

Learn how to use all of the resources for inventory management that is going to make clarified actions with the products that you choose to dropship. The company will be profiting as a whole but there needs to be an anchor of brand establishment with the product like having full transparency to the customer basis in demand. The product development within the company's supply is going to evolve with the future of the customer basis. With some customers, the business is going to learn that the customer will have new requests for both general and detail-specific products.

With new requests, the company is going to have fulfilled the needs of their clients because they have purchased dedicated for long. There needs to be consistency for the entirety of the client basis. With product diversity, there is going to bring new demands for the product suppliers. Suppliers are going to have performed to new standards and there will be new heights that the company and the supplier will have to reach together. These concerns and demands need to be mentioned beforehand and they need to be communicated to the supplier in advance so that there is complete transparency.

The supplier is going to be aware of every concern the dropshipping e-commerce site will have and they will perform well for the shop. The shop will become a more manageable place when there is stability with the decisions that are made and when there are more tracking and invoice management. Everything will need to be on the books and that includes the extra notes for extra transactions done within the fiscal month. The suppliers are going to engage with you in manners that you will only find out once you interact with them.

Some suppliers are not going to be so nice to deal with and it needs to be made aware of early on in the Dropshipping dedication to these suppliers. If there is a supplier that does not represent themselves in a well-natured manner, the company is going to be doing bad business real fast by sending thousands of dollars there way and getting poor cooperation in return. Eliminate bad suppliers and this is going to be a great tactic for the company owner to get to know the products that are in the shop.

Get to know your products and every value that it brings the customers and the market around your shop. There may come a point when the company frees up assets. These assets can be used to make serious moves with company and branding. We can even consider the possibility that the company can even include some of the company's self-branded products in the product line. There can be products made now with the companies name on it and this could get company advertising.

These direct advertising tactics are going to cause new territory advancements and this will include new communities finding out about the new product lines that are now online. Suppliers will be able to negotiate prices with you about creating this customized product for your line. Since there will be a dedication to the company they will be more than willing to work with the dropshipping site on a more personalized level. Make new moves and get to know your product so that you know where the company is going to advance every quarter that comes.

The Fulfilment of the Customers Is The First Priority

Fulfilling customer orders is the priority and especially for customers that are ordering on a recurring schedule. These customers are going to be a strong backbone to the business structure as it is going to create buyer-security. By having buyer-security the revenue will always be achieved on a weekly or monthly basis. The fulfillment customers are going to need a schedule to fulfill their orders because they are not going to just be on the margins of the agenda

The business owner needs to prioritize every single fulfillment customer especially and more than just the one-time buyers that aren't bringing weekly profits. These profits of the individuals are good but every quarter the other companies who the owner fulfills possible massive quantities to. This is going to be crucial for the company's growth into the next variety of customer satisfaction.

New clients will have new demands and the company must take them on swiftly while they are handling the long term customers that have been well established before we have begun to look at the new client base there is now. The company will handle every fulfillment with a strategy that creates an important role focus that sheds onto the customer.

Fulfilling the daily needs of the customer is going to become an automated task. The company owner cannot handle every request from every buyer to the shop. There must be an automated system at play so it alleviates the workload of the business owner and it allows them to handle the business universally. Every task will be automated for the owner and they will be able to move the PO's through at a faster rate.

Every PO needs to maintain a quick timestamp that is a clarification to the buyer and the seller that the transaction had occurred with specific details. Every customer needs to get an email that is a clarification that they did or did not get the package. This email needs to come with a tracking code or tracking slip that can tell the buyer when the package is going to finally arrive.

How to Differentiate You From the Competitions

Separate yourselves from the rest of the shop community because there is going to be some competition that plays seriously. Be ready to establish your mark in the global e-commerce community so you can have that strong impact on the buyers to fall back on. Lead the mark with good products and good product assistance while the dropshipping is getting ramped up. Communicate with sellers differently and optimize messages to be personalized to the customers that are trying to purchase products.

Give feedback on your client's requests so that they know you are engaged with knowing exactly what they are interested in buying. Most of the clients buy in bulk and that is how the personalization of the product choice can be modified to better suit each customer. Every customer is going to have a customizable PO or

Purchase Order is going to be made for the company to company interaction so that it can be kept documented for further statements and it will surely make the company stand out from the rest.

This is also a good time to create digital welcome cards or print new business cards that can be distributed possibly through a mailing subscription list or through the public venues that can also remark as a public advertisement. Have a great attitude and bring a great personal note to the online presence that is made. Bring positivity to the shop environment will go a long way. Having a great attitude on the shop will rub off onto the business clients that became more acquainted to buying.

Strenuous work might be something that separates you from the pack because there are a lot of companies that try the set it and forget it attitude and this often only gets them sales or practically fractions of sales. The best are in going to generally put in the most work. The more drive someone as they will just see more profits and potential moves to be made. Simple concepts like this go can take someone far as long as the two coincide with their drive into their business drive.

Create a local drive that separates all of the competition so that brand marketing can shine. Brand marketing is the way to the people's home and it's going to be through great marketing and personalizing every PO and shop order to fit the needs of the customer. Customers are going to love the brand more and more if they see the name of the shop on their receipts. Utilize receipt tracking to have PO's sent to the client's phone or contact line so that they can document or manifest their tracking slips in an instant. This will increase buyer flow as the company will be able to handle more workload at once.

Automation is going to be one of the things that separate this company from the others and that is by optimizing customer supplying experience. Customers that have a great experience with their products will come back for more and that is certain. Some companies create product value but it is crucial to have quality values that can stand beside these great companies. Automation is going to create an easier working atmosphere while the business owner will remain free to be doing other tasks in their day or even sleeping and getting a full nights rest.

Chapter 7: How to Handle Security Issues with Business Strategy

Select A Platform that is Secure

There are going to be risks that come with creating an online shop that generates great amounts of revenue. There will be attacks on the assets of the company and its site that will render the assets of the company and they could take away everything that the owner has all from a push of a button. This is a harsh reality but we must protect all assets against these types of advances to our capital. There are platforms on the web that are going to protect the assets from intruders that are going to try and take the information.

There is valuable information that the company will take if the assets are not protected. These assets can include personal information and billing information like addresses and even possible phone numbers that can be listed on the accounts. These types of information are taken from the public and they are sold so it is viable that the companies protect this information along with the importance of their assets. A secure platform is going to have an encrypted system that helps your system as a basic shield for attackers to yield from.

These protected servers are going to have great malware that is protecting the encrypted passwords and databases from malicious attacks that cannot penetrate the shield to decode. A secure platform will let any supplier know that there are going to be updated to the security firewall or that if they need to charge for more space to secure there can be pricing organizing. Pay for your protection under secure connections and trusted servers so that you can dropship in peace and know that your database is safe. Safety is the most important factor for keeping trusting buyers to visit our accounts and put in their information to process for our shipping systems.

Set Higher Standards For Passwords

Make a great password list for your accounts and have a secretive system for choosing where to keep these files and what they are going to be. It is great to use multiple characters and using apostrophes or dashes and exclamation marks. Make a password with mixed characters that are also mixed with numbers that are complicated and write it down or document it somewhere that will have a permanent place and it will not get lost. Make a password that no one can guess and with no words that are naturally words and with meaning.

Password with not too many consecutive numbers instead a great mix of all of the characters and it will be set with your account. Create a password keychain possibly for an easier way to get through many different tiers of the business system. You can give each employee or holder a specific password for the keychain that will all tie into the main password and that will be a tracker for administrative action.

Protection Against Any DDoS Attacks

There are going to be attacked on the servers and it is going to slow down many processes on each of the accounts that are running including the shop. Identify any DDoS attack as early as possible and if you run your servers, then you need to be able to monitor every single status point to see when or when not you are under attack. Critical timing making the sooner you can recognize that problem with your website is due to an attack the sooner you can wipe out the

DDoS attack. This attack is going to be nothing but a threat to secure information those customers new and long term been giving information.

To get into the mode of this it's good practice to familiarize yourself with a typical inbound traffic profile because the more you know about what your normal traffic looks like. It will be easy to spot when its profile changes. Most DDoS attacks make sharp spikes in traffic and learning these great habits to be able to tell the difference between a sudden eruption of incoming legitimate visiting crowds and the start of a DDoS attack.

It's a good idea about nominating a DDoS leader in your company who is responsible for acting should you come under attack. This will create a provisional status for the company and its bystanders.

Allocating bandwidth

Overprovisioning bandwidth comes with distributing total numbers of writes and erases across huge and huger populations of flash blocks and pages over time. It makes sense to have more bandwidth available to your Web server than you need. That way, you can accommodate the mixed varieties of surges in traffic that could be a result of an advertising campaign or a mention that came indirectly to the site at one point or another. Welcome these traffic hikes and you are going to keep trending.

Overprovision by doubling or even quadrupling bandwidth still won't likely stop a DDoS attack. But if you act accordingly it could spare a moment to act with the conscious flow a few extra before any resources are overwhelmed and might go out of order. Set lower SYN and UDP flood drop thresholds for our next routes. Always stay close to the network parameter with any means of defense. There some great technical precautions that can be taken to somewhat mitigate the effect of an attack -- especially in the first minutes so think about some tips.

Rate limit your router to prevent your Web server from being overwhelmed
add filters to optimize the personal router to drop packets from obvious sources of attack and this will populate. Drop timeout half-open connections more aggressively
drop spoofed or malformed packages. This is going to create more processing speed and allocate bandwidth. Although these precautions have been effective in the past, DDoS attacks are now usually too large for these measures to be able to stop a DDoS attack in complete. This is likely only going to buy the company site more time before the attack will ramp up and become more aggressive to the servers.

Call Your ISP or Hosting Provider

The next step is to call your ISP or the specific hosting provider if you don't the server and tell them you are under attack and wait for their suggestion on how to handle this attack. Keep emergency contacts for your ISP or hosting provider available so you can act as quickly as possible during any circumstance keeping in mind that an attack could happen anywhere. If it is possible to set alerts on the cell phone or personal electronic device precautions can be made to have alerts made for the owner.

A good ISP or host may already have detected it a strong attack but it may not be detected if it is only the beginning. If the attack is on their servers themselves they may even find themselves overwhelmed by the attack. This could mean that there are going to be longer service request times. Servers possibly will have a backup or they will be restored within hours of a crash.

Have a host manage the account for any precaution to a DDoS attack because it will be the more secure option for any new dropship especially. Their data center will likely have exceedingly higher bandwidth links and higher capacity routers and the company will also have way more experience dealing with attacks. Web servers located with a data center will also keep DDoS traffic aimed at your Web server of your corporate LAN so email and possibly voice over IP (VoIP) services will still have full functionality even if an attack is undergone. To get the website back online your ISP or hosting company may divert traffic to a "scrubber" where the malicious server packets can be removed before the legitimate ones are going to be routed to your Web server.

The first objective to these service providers is when they see a customer under attack is to log onto their routers and stop the traffic from getting onto the network. It takes minutes practically to propagate globally using BGP or Border Gateway Protocol and traffic will fall off rapidly. It's costly for a hosting company to allow a DDoS onto their network because it consumes bandwidth and even affects customers and the site might even risk getting blackholed by the web server.

The company is going to protect every server by using various tools to understand how the traffic to sites are changing from seeing what it was received before and by identifying malicious packets that threaten the servers. Service providers can take in and scrub to send on very high levels of traffic and considering the high levels of traffic that are out there like the social media accounts that host marketplaces or social messaging services alike.

Creating the DDoS Playbook

Time-critical steps and methods are taken to stop a DDoS attack. Create a playbook that documents in many details all steps of a pre-planned response to an attack that is being detected in the days or minutes coming. DDoS mitigation companies simulate DDoS attacks; organizing many ways for you to develop and refine a corporate procedure for reacting to a real attack that can cost practically thousands had it be real attacks. Even just being a fake attack it will be the clearest thing to mimic such an attack.

Simulating fake attacks will create security awareness for the company as a unit and there will be no part of the sector that is caught off guard when the attack hits; there will be full team cooperation to move the company through the imminent attack. There must be a call to arms when this attack comes because it is not something a company can take lying down. Stand up with affirmative action and trace every source this attack can be coming from because it can be risking the solidarity of the company's online structure. DDoS stands for Distributed Denial of Service and this can be a criminal offense.

Don't stand for this when there is an attack because the company is going to need to move fast and keep their inventory safe from risks. Competitors could be attacking you to bring down your ad powers and this is not going to be good for business. Do not participate in these bad habits because they are also criminal offenses that no one needs to follow.

There may need to be an emergency plan if there is no way to get the site running again in case of a DDoS attack the business is going to need to run strong. Many servers can support your data but there needs to be a good search for reliable support. Look in the right places and feel free to ask questions to the service providers that you are thinking of creating a payment plan with.

An important part of your planned response to a DDoS attack is that communication with the customers about this problem will be crucial. DDoS attacks can last as long as 24 hours, and good communication can assure your customers that their orders are in good hands. It is important to make the customer feel valued so this is the last time to forget about the feelings of the customer. We want to bring assurance and appreciation when it comes to displaying shop core values because it must be known that the customer will also appreciate being treated this way. The customer is always right and we always have to make the right decisions to come to a healthy balance in the e-commerce world.

Get In Touch With a DDoS Mitigation Expert

For larger attacks on the company's server, it is your best chance of staying
Online by using a specialist DDoS mitigation company for your requests. These organizations have large-scale infrastructure and manage great technologies involving data scrubbing that keeps a constant connected online website. Contact a DDoS mitigation company directly and search your hosting company/ service provider that may have a partnership agreement with services to handle larger attacks on their servers.

Different server scrubbing center can handle very high levels of traffic and sends on the cleansed traffic to the intended destination. This organization results in higher latency for website users and their process free up, being the alternative that there wouldn't be any access to the site at all. Subscribing to a DDoS mitigation service on an annual basis may cost a couple of hundred dollars a month. If you wait until you need one and expect to pay much more for the service and wait longer before it starts to work its magic.

DDoS mitigation services are going to come with a cost and it's essentially up to you whether you're willing to pay to stay online or take the hit and wait for the DDoS attack to subside before your opportunity to do business again.

DDoS mitigation specialists include. These are some listed services that are very qualified at protecting the rights and external and internal resources for Dropshipping companies and web domains alike.

Mitigation Companies

1. Akamai DDoS mitigation

2. Verisign DDoS Protection Services

3. Radware DDoS Protection

4. Cloudflare DDoS Protection

5. F5 DDoS Protection

6. Imperva Incapsula

Use an SSL Protection Layer

SSL certificates create an encrypted connection and establish trust.

One of the most important components of online business is creating a trusted environment where potential customers feel confident in making purchases. SSL certificates create a foundation of trust by establishing a secure connection. To assure visitors their connection is secure, browsers provide special visual cues that we call EV indicators -- anything from a green padlock to branded URL bar.

SSL certificates have a key pair: a public and a private key. These keys work together to establish an encrypted connection. The certificate also contains what is called the "subject," which is the identity of the certificate/website owner.

To get a certificate, you must create a Certificate Signing Request (CSR) on your server. This process creates a private key and public key on your server. The CSR data file that you send to the SSL Certificate issuer (called a Certificate Authority or CA) contains the public key. The CA uses the CSR data file to create a data structure to match your private key without compromising the key itself. The CA never sees the private key. Once you receive the SSL certificate, you install it on your server. You also install an intermediate certificate that establishes the credibility of your SSL Certificate by tying it to your CA's root certificate. The instructions for installing and testing your certificate will be different depending on your server.

The most important part of an SSL certificate is that it is digitally signed by a trusted CA, like DigiCert. Anyone can create a certificate, but browsers only trust certificates that come from an organization on their list of trusted CAs. Browsers come with a pre-installed list of trusted CAs, known as the Trusted Root CA store. To be added to the Trusted Root CA store and thus become a Certificate Authority, a company must comply with and be audited against security and authentication standards established by the browsers.

An SSL Certificate issued by a CA to an organization and its domain/website verifies that a trusted third party has authenticated that organization's identity. Since the browser trusts the CA, the browser now trusts that organization's identity too. The browser lets the user know that the website is secure, and the user can feel safe browsing the site and even entering their confidential information.

Chapter 8: How to Scale-Up Your Business

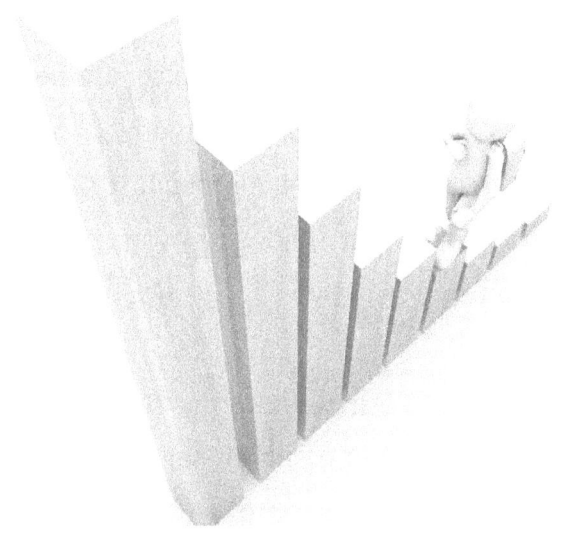

Add More Products to Your Inventory and Consider Seasonal Items

Seasonal events come every year and this is a perfect opportunity to get the most out of the yearly sales. Easter sales, Black Friday sales, and Christmas sales alike are the hosting days for some of the biggest sales of the year. It's important to stay on top every day of the year so you can prepare for what is to come these holidays. Seasonal promotions are what some people are waiting for and finally getting to see these deals are going to be their moment of happiness and purchase. Everyone is getting gifts this year and as the company, it must step in at the right time and show value when it matters most.

Consistent sales are going to drive the company forward and this is proven on sales reports. The best part about going into seasonal selling is having that consistency beforehand ensuring that the company practically doubles in profit going into this new season. For bulk buyers everyone these good deals are going to be sought for so that good deals can be made and they can also get the most bangs for their bucks. Some companies only find their niche when it's already the holiday season. They make profit happen to make up for the rest of the fiscal year not having any incoming revenue. This kind of company will only generate seasonal money and you should instead see seasonal time as a time to optimize and maximize sales.

There may be a fun event or a team building event that is coming that you can also sponsor your product during. An event may arise and you will be able to showcase the event with your products and spread brand awareness to drive more traffic to your shop site. There may be a very specific event that correlates with your product and for a good exposure, the business will take this venture and use their product to create brand awareness. This could include for example an expose where merchants gather to sell their goods. The host deals offline at events like per se an expo to drive more traffic to your e-commerce site and has exclusive deals that can only be found at certain times or venues.

This will be organic traffic and will bring in serious customers that are most likely to purchase. Showcase special items that are on times schedules so that there is a limited time offer value that is not always around. Customers will come from fat to get into this time window and they will purchase until the window is gone.

Tactics like this will generate quick sales in a small amount of time that will leave some of your buyers in amazement until they come to shop again. Utilize these simple tips to generate more revenue for the dropshipping business and find out who is going to buy during the holidays. It is a good way to start the seasons with a holiday and the business needs to make it bright and giving for the customer and first-time visitors to get the most out of this coming season.

Hire Others Collaborators to Help You Manage The Business

Things may have been running just as smoothly as you expected to and increasing productions there may have been a concept proposed to hire a new employee or welcome a new collaboration into your vision. When numbers go up they go up and this is no time to sit down and relax. If productions are ramping up and the business is ready to make it serious well when it is time to hire someone willing to succeed. This hire could be any you choose but choose wisely as this is not any other business. This is a Dropshipping business that requires attention and skill.

You cannot just hire anybody that says they can do the job. If you are not hiring for package handling then you may be hiring to help with the online work and these are both very sensitive positions. The business owner will be dealing with a lot of sensitive data and personal information from the customers of the shop. They are going to have access to almost all of the assets as long as you as the administrator remember your role. Administrators do not hand their responsibilities or clearance to anyone. It takes a strong leader with their vision of quality e-commerce to paint a perfect picture.

To lead the right team takes the best motivation and in any team, there needs to be collaboration. There needs to be one hundred percent transparency so that if any issues arise that it will be solved within a moment's notice. As well there needs to be this honesty because this team will be also making new decisions to ramp up productions further and everyone needs to be on the same page. If there are disagreements this usually leads to the administrator of the shop site kicking the newbie off of the team. As a team member newbie tell your leader what to do or expect yourself on the curb looking for a new job because the assets are of the owners only. They will be making ultimate decisions on their accounts as an administrator.

This could be time for a change and if the tide is rising to your neck already then it's time to hire a helper. Let us just say right now good help is not cheap so this is not a step to take until you can surely finance. There have been too many companies with locked doors and angry laid-off workers outside the warehouses. It is timed to change this from happening and represent a strong and powerful company that is ready to lead.

We are talking about a Dropshipping company so thank gosh there isn't going to be warehouse costs associated with the company name. With the greatness of Dropshipping, the best part is that you don't need to hire a full teamed staff to run your business while you are handling the odds and ends as the business owner. Dropshipping makes it easier to run the business from the front lines picking your specific clientele.

This is a revolutionary business that can be managed from one source, one computer, and one desk. What more can one ask for when they think to hire extra help and all they need is just one extra employee? This will be the life but the company will need to make sure that they compensate them every penny earned for their specific tasks.

Chapter 9: How to Dropship with Shopify

Dropshipping with Shopify is somewhat like dropshipping on any other site but we will list the rewards that also come with purchasing their advanced Shopify. With this service provider, the Dropshipping routine will be the same mostly all around and there will be the basics to complete the tasks. The company is going to order a product and the supplier of the product is going to begin shipments and packing. The product goes directly to the warehouse and the supplier sends the package directly to the warehouse which soon will be making its way to the customer that ordered.

There are the basic essential steps you will need with Shopify and there will be different rates for different plans. Shopify also allows the dropshipper to make up to fifteen staff accounts and these could be for any extra faculties or back up accounts that the owner will need to set up. There are great discount codes and the purchase of services comes with a free SSL certificate. Shopify offers care abandonment recovery for any shoppers that may have had a link time out and lose their shopping cart and their hard work of finding everything that they wanted.

The free SSL certificate will create more privacy for the company's sensitive information and will encrypt the code for the main users on the account. Shopify will print shipping labels and will supply USPS Priority Mail Cubic pricing. Shopify comes with its app. This will make it for many dropshippers to use the selling program from the palm of their hand which can make every process a whole lot easier. The app can do mostly everything the desktop can. It will also give alert notifications to the personal device when there is something new happening with the shop or any of its orders that it is keeping track of.

Using Shopify is going to personalize the experience that selling will bring and depending on the rate and system that you choose it could suit the business for all it needs. Fully interact with every addition that the system offers to maximize profit goals. Take on everything that Shopify offers so that you can fully experience what they have to offer. Shopify is a trusted source for many dropshippers in the global scene and it has a strong reputation that stands in front of all of the shops it represents. It is crucial for the company to pick a service provider that has a good reputation so the entirety of the shop will have a strong backing to its name.

Chapter 10: How to Dropship on Amazon and eBay

Dropshipping On Amazon

Dropshipping with Amazon is great and it is just another good service provider to sell products with. Selecting a service provider like Amazon will also include FBA and also FBA Fulfillment. When a Dropshipping company decides to go with Amazon for its product distribution it will open a few doors. First of all, Amazon handles all of the shipping and handling that goes into delivering the product. Amazon is going to pack and weigh all of the items and record all metrics into their system for data tracking.

The company will need to purchase electronic product storage space and also the time amount that they want the shop to be running on the internet. The space to sell will be paid for as long as the company keeps getting consistent sales with the product line. FBA will fulfill all of the needs that the customer has with FBA fulfillment. With this set in place, selling times and schedules can be optimized in many ways to handle recurring transactions and even personalized PO's from company to company. FBA fulfillment is going to keep track of all clients that buying on a routine basis by organizing their needs and the Dropshipping schedules that have been made to fulfill.

Amazon weighs the product per pound. These rates apply to any of the products shipped so there can be a good spending system at play for moving different varieties of the product value. As Amazon states, "Make sure the products are e-commerce ready."

This means that the company must make sure that the products they are going to be selling are practically already online and they are in a queue that is going to sell fast. One of the cool things is that Amazon will let you ship your products to them and the company can begin selling their company-branded items that are going to be great marketing for the company

Amazon also provides customer support for all of the customers and orders that are placed with the company. If there is anything that goes wrong with the package during shipment Amazon will contact both the buyer and the seller to keep full awareness of what is going on. This is a great play because most people know the name Amazon and they trust this name. It is important to stand with a trusted company if the company at hand has no name for itself. Although a few followers on the social accounts is great and shows effort it makes it all the much easier to dropship having a multimillion dollar company backing you up with professional labeling and a reputation that keep the company grounded.

Dropshipping on eBay

Dropshipping with eBay works the same way as with Amazon but there are different benefits like having bidding structures. These selling techniques can welcome new sellers that have different product value and are looking for rare items. They use the same time of hosting platform. The business owner just purchases inventory space but there must be a good part on the seller if there is going to be a custom product sold. Dropshippers communicate with many distributors and this is how they can supply such a diverse market.

Chapter 11: Creating a Personal Website for Your Dropshipping Business

Get Your Domain Name And Web Hosting

Establish a domain name and pay for web hosting under a certain server. Pay for yearly access and establish an online shop to a global market with many tips to optimize your market. Having a domain name is going to establish the internal location that your customers are going to recognize when they look at the top of the search engine to know they are at your shop. Having a strong and simple domain name will attract others to be able to type the name in them and willingly want to search the site rather than randomly come across it in the search engine.

Install WordPress

Install WordPress as it is going to be one of the only platforms that help you write scripts online that establish a connection to your shop and the online world. WordPress can be downloaded for free online and there just needs to be a trusted link. The pros of WordPress are that you will be able to fully optimize your website and its components with just a few adjustments. It is a scriptwriter that can internally place your website in a specific way to attract viewers and make the interactions easier for buyers when they are checking out.

Set Up the Website And Pick The Right Plugins

Establish a great website that displays the shop's aesthetics and makes sure that it shines. It is going to need the right plugins like those of Wordpress to make the site run interactively and great for the consumer to have a great experience in the shop. There are plugins on the market that are going to have components that resemble some of the competitor's sites. These are going to be used to advantage when marketing to a certain audience. This is going to be crucial for customers that are browsing items for specific brands where they are going to be used to a certain structure. It will be profitable to attain and implement these same selling widgets and plugins.

Chapter 12: Social Media Approach in Dropshipping

Social Media Marketing approach

A successful business does well marketing on public streets but the truth is since we are entering a new age of electronic future businesses must make haste for their change if they haven't gotten to it yet. This next change is to discover the new world of social media marketing. You are going to be reaching out online in many different ways. If there has been any previous advertisement experience had for the business then one knows the power the word of mouth can bring.

Having social interactions with others build a great rapport with the individuals engaged. This kind of behavior is going to promote the global presence that the e-commerce shop has.

Bringing in social media to an already online and trending topic is going to make with e-commerce a perfect pair. A business might have more than half of their following on a social media scale and thus in great odds will also make it easier to combine them into some good business marketing.

Bring the business to the front lines and where more than half the customers are; that's online. The web is going to be a strong motivator for content you are going to design your product line. Release a post about your new inventory and be descriptive when you tell the world that is going to pop and be a strong reminder to the visitors why they are going to visit your shop and ultimately why they will buy. Get started now and try making a social media account if you do not have one already.

There are tons of providers and many of them you will be able to market your business with. Create a login and finish editing the personal information on the account and everything that the business will be displaying to the public. Make the business account look nice and professional and it will attract business-like followers ready to see your catalog. Choose a provider that fits your needs or open two or many accounts to see which is going to work best for the business. The business owner may choose one social media outlet over another and this could give the business presence edge.

The only way to tell the right fit is to just jump right in and start designing. Social media has strong sources of the population that are willing to third-party market and this is why it's important to establish a bond with the community that surrounds. It can city-based or global to give back in many ways as long as you make the connection with your audience. Make their time worthwhile since they are spending so much online searching. Supply an online incentive that will encourage your audience to come back and share the content with other friends and family that are with them on these accounts. Find important partners that can also give you mentions and that will give you credible posts about the business you run and for many to see.

The question is can the e-commerce website survive from only social media marketing. This is not going to be a likely route because the only option the business has could lose it and have nothing left for support. If the company only dedicated their marketing budget to social media marketing, they are going to see the expensive cost burn through the budget quickly. Popularity is so important when it comes to running an efficiently visited shop but the company needs to take advantage of its capabilities to obtain followers from the social media sites that they could also be using, some of them even being free.

The more popularity you have the more profitable the business can be. The business can create very engaging motives towards their audience and they could attract more and more attention to the sites that are trickling into the shop daily. Keep gaining more followers and see what this popularity can do for the business.

Facebook Ads

Facebook ads are great and they are for any age range with a company structure. With Facebook as a company can market themselves from the bottom up and with little to no cost at all. Running Facebook ads can become costly if there is no following audience to broadcast to. If the company has no following on their websites then they are going to be paying money for company promotion and not for product promotion depending on how far we have gotten already.

These social ads are great because it engages thousands of people together for a common focus on the marketplace and this creates a strong playing field for posting products on any page. A company can pay for personalized ads that are going to air for the community to see sponsored posts on their pages and feeds so that they cleverly run into company products posted for great values. These advertisements cost the company upfront but they will also give great exposure to the presence of the shop.

The shop can post an ad about its new items or maybe marked down items that the company has extra inventory of. If the company can make an ad about the marked down items that are full in the inventory warehouse then products can be efficiently moved off of the warehouse shelves and into new revenue that is going to have the company break even with its assets. There has to be a balanced routine when it comes to paying for Facebook ads because not only can they get pricey but there will also be other ads that bring competition to the playing board.

It is in the best interest of the company to know exactly when to place an ad on the market. The company is going to need to be ready for any turnover and sales to skyrocket if necessary because if there is the right product niche the success is going to come pouring out. Customize ads with the company logo and titles that entice the customers to come on in and visit for the new sales. There is going to be opportunities to make a catalog or a flip advertisement and get creative with the cover flow when putting up an advertisement for the week.

Advertise on a good schedule so that none of the customers see the posts as spam and give the audience a chance to respond to the advertisement and give feedback about the current promotion. Utilize these ads when holidays come around and make an advertisement that speaks out above news in the Facebook place. This Facebook marketplace is going to create a level opportunity to see your posts and engage with the shop site that you like to involve in the posts. Ads can also be placed on the Facebook marketplace and this could include single items or bulk items.

This is a not usually the case because there are at times selling restrictions under certain sites but with Facebook ads this allows the company to list any variety of products. The company will be able to list products that can be sold as common goods or rare goods that are even handmade and at a limited source. Take advantage of the market diversity within Facebook because it will create a great opportunity to post and post again even when the product may not have sold the first week. If the product does not sell the first week through a Facebook ad markup the price and make the product bio look spiffier.

When the customers see that ad again they will have a new take on it and they will dedicate more time to considering visiting the shop site and picking out something that encouraged them to get there. With Facebook ads, it will be easier and easier for the average product supplier to have a global reach for the line in their shop. Global diversity is important so that every market genre can be tapped into and the company can take full advantage of selling their products to everyone around the world never missing a sale.

Google Adwords

With Google Adwords, there is going to be great diversity in search engines to bring plenty of crowds to the consumer website. With Google, Adwords google is going to place ads for the company on several landing servers and it is going to create ad space for all sites that are affected. Adwords is going to display ads for the company that relates to the company's mission or its makeup so that when someone is shopping or researching a site low and behold there will be an ad for the company and its product. This company ad is going to replace any space that may not have had an ad in the first place and this will create brand marketing for anyone who sees this ad.

Adwords control the ads that individuals see when they conduct searches like google searches for a specific product. This search is going to bring up many trending topics and depending on how much money the company decided to spend with AdWords the trending topic could the shop on a seasonal weekend. If the company is just starting Adwords is going to make a great opener for a company that has not built any brand advertisement. Lead a great advertising campaign by setting some money aside and spending it on advertisements every quarter to create a better-defined presence online.

This is going to maximize the reach the company makes on all of the audiences and this is going to ramp up production for any customers that have not seen or purchased from the shop yet. If product awareness can be brought to attention for the viewers all at once there could be a high spike of customers that come in to purchase all at once and this could send the company into a new stratosphere of sales. One of the main consistencies is the crowd flow and the amount of advertisement money spent which could be with Google Adwords.

Chapter 13: How Amazon FBA Can Help You Grow Your Business

Approach to Amazon FBA system

Fulfillment by Amazon is going to be a helpful tool for the company to utilize for future growth with dropshipping. Dropshipping with fulfillment is going to alleviate stresses on packing and shipping the products to the customers. Usually, the seller has to pack the package and make it safely shippable to send off to the customer which can be costly for the seller if there are many shipments going at once. One of the best parts of FBA is that if there are many shipments that are doubled up or if the many customers are on the same shipping zone.

These many shipments can be sent out at once and this could minimize on shipping costs so much that it is going to keep revenue in the company than letting it trickle out by cents and cents by making individual shipments. Creating an automated system for all of the shipments that are being placed is going to make it easier for the company owner to establish to cornerstones with the company. Automating the recurring shipments to take place for the customers that have weekly requests will make it easier on the company to sell to the individual customers that come into the shop to buy.

With FBA some of the shipments fulfilled can even get eligibility for the products to have free shipping. With Amazon FBA this shipping will be prime shipping and it can qualify for items that are specific price ranges. Amazon will charge the company to keep its products listed on their site and it will be a flat rate for any type of inventory. If the company builds up a great rapport with FBA they can receive more prime shipping on their shop offers.

One of the main advantages of participating in Amazon FBA is going to be standing behind a company that is so reputable already. The establishment has done very well for itself and this is why many companies choose to sell with Amazon. Amazon will support their clients and that is why it is good to let trust in for this system to go above and beyond for the company as you would for your own.

Amazon is going to also boost customer traffic to the company's products being the fact that they are on Amazon's website and will be in the mix of the thousands other quality items that they choose to represent. Choose Amazon FBA to look like a trending brand ready to sell out the gate because Amazon is going to have great product representation and they are going to give great customer support whenever the dropshipping business will need an extra hand in customer management.

Chapter 14: How to Dropship in the Practical Way and How to Sell Effectively Your Products

Open the Horizon

When the business is well underway this is going to be a perfect time to open the playing field for further outreach. Your customers are going to be happy with the service already provided but there needs to be constant attention to the customers and they need to be presented with new things and new products from time to time that can remind them why they came to find us in the first place. The horizon is bright and with your product line, there are a thousand ways to paint this picture. Invite customers to refer friends to the page and give incentives for whoever participates.

If there is a customer who refers 5 or more friends go ahead and give them 15% off for the whole month and witness how much your customer will enjoy these perks. There are going to be many ways to keep your audience engaged with the products because we have to remember they need to be purchasing and not just coming to your site for a quick visit. Do not let your audience go unattended or they will take their business elsewhere so keep them engaged with some words of appreciation or extra incentives to come back and shop at the site again.

Create a rewards system like Shopify offers with gift cards and establish an earning-based point system that allows customers to rack up points in the shop for every dollar spent. With the more money, they spend with the company the more products they will be able to redeem for value or purchase. This is going to bring in special customers that are looking to get back more than just a couple simple purchases with the shop because these customers will most likely appreciate the value that the company brings and the offers that stand apart from the competition.

Competition is okay with this day and age so as long as it does not negatively affect profits there can be many strategies set in motion that are going to take the company a long way in their online presence. The stronger the online presence the more someone will shop at a site so we must remember to keep out site looking pretty and with nifty tricks or buttons that are going to give a great customer experience from the moment they arrive at the moment of purchase. Creating greater customer experiences with these customers is going to attract more customers that are like minded and there will begin to become a common interest at the shop.

If there is a theme setting in this will be the time to capitalize on it and bring in more customers.

Do not leave the shop looking the boring same after years and years of selling because the customers like to be wooed with new templates and engaging web spaces that they can spend their time. Although it may just seem like a customer is coming to spend money on the shop it must also be made aware that they are coming to the shop to also spend their time and involve themselves with something new. Make sure your shop is safe and giving space for your community.

If the customers are spending just a few or maybe even a few hours on the site that they are going to enjoy every second and they are not going to find a reason to make them want to leave. A great site is going to anchor the buyer and this will create constant sales. For a successful dropshipping business it is safe to say there need to be constant sales because there are going to be fees are services to pay for all of the online activity being conducted. Have great standards for the dropshipping website and put yourself in the shoes of the customer so that you are confident in knowing what exactly your customer needs and how you are going to supply the greatest possible assistance to get it to them.

Selling exclusively can become a profitable endeavor but we have to make sure that our products are only as exclusive as we make them. There are going to be buyers from our shop that request a very specific product and let's just say for the right price you can be the one to get it to them. Listing products online is going to be great if there are bulk sales and if sales are flying out the door and one thing we must make sure is that one buyer is not purchasing the entire inventory that is going to be processed through PO for another buyer.

We must have constant organization and the willingness to stock the proper amount of inventory. If there is also a customer that comes to us for the specific goods we must remember to make a dedicated space for them in our books so that we never fail to fulfill an order with this customer. These customers are going to be dealing exclusively with the company product line so in that respect, the company should also be dealing with them exclusively to solidify these trades. Products that are not common goods are going to be sought at a high price at times and it may even require the company owner to go through extra means to obtain the inventory for its clients.

This isn't going to come cheap if you have expensive exporting rates and high inventory rates for the bulk items on the warehouse floor. Charge a good price and don't be afraid to negotiate this price to a reasonable level of understanding for both the buyer and the seller. Let the buyer know you are giving them a better deal than anything else they are going to find at other sources and represent a good product to back up these statements.

Send out shipments that are on correlating shipping paths at the same time or on the same routes and save more money on shipping services. If FBA is in place leave the hard parts to the distributors and take reigns to stir your company in the right directions. There is a possible loss of complete control for the dropshipping business here but it is not going to take away the say-so of the company owner so there should be no worry completing these monthly fees for the services that run the dropshipping company.

Create firewalls as lines of defense for the business livelihood because there are going to be attackers out there that want to see the shop crumble. Some of these threats might be electronic and more advanced than human error or human hackers so it is very crucial that any

DDoS attack that comes will be handled within a minutes notice and there will be precautions to mask this attack from its full force. Be prepared for the hack by joining with great companies like Shopify that will supply the company their very own SSL certificate which is going to protect their encrypted links from any malicious behaviors on the net.

Do not risk a complete site crash and just settle for the SSL otherwise there is going to be packets dropped onto the company site and it is going to make it near impossible to just ride the attack out. There is a possibility they can seize all practical assets from the company site if the hacker knows what they are doing. Remember that these attacks are going to halt all purchasing on the accounts and that your customers, in the end, will suffer. Being prepared is the best measure of defense because the company will be at its strongest point if there ever did become an attack.

Indirect Marketing

There are many ways to the indirect market and the customers are going to become one of the main ways that your brand gets advertisement. Sure we can spend money on Facebook ads and this will get us some impressions on the community but there is nothing better than a customer mentioning to their friend where they made their last purchase and the fact that if that customer refers a friend to come in and shop as well they will receive discount codes.

Creating value for the customer is going to be one of the main reasons they do come back to shop again. Send out emails or even physical mail with your company name on the envelope or create a welcome message that welcomes each and every customer back to the shop by their first name. This is going to give great marketing value because it is not so complicated to do most of these things and to see the return will be exponential.

Look for ways to break the mold and grab the attention of all the customers in the area and if that means posting an ad on a Facebook and then make it a great post and put one of your new products on it with only a few words of memorable acknowledgment. You can create a newsletter that states that the shop is so happy to have great movement in the last quarter and that the shop will be celebrating its 2nd year anniversary. These are all engaging things to bring the community into to make them feel like they are part of the everlasting change that has shown great results.

Product Management

Manage your products with great detail and make sure that there are not too many duplicate products that do not stand out from the product line as a whole. This is going to be important for individuals that are going to be looking through every product in the line and trying to decide on which specifics to choose from or to buy in bulk. Make sure the products all stand out so that every product can also stand alone in the shop and still generate sales. Stand behind good products that are going to be used and purchased again and never underestimate the power of quality.

There are going to be hundreds of suppliers out there to choose from but it's going to be up to the company owner to pick and choose the very right fit for the quality of the shop. The quality of the product line is essentially going to affect the appearance of the shop to the community. Stand behind quality just as you would in the personnel office and make sure that every package is being sent out efficiently and on time.

Consistency

Stay consistent with all sales and keep pushing for the quarterly sales goals. This is going to ensure that the company is on a constant up rise and there will be revenue made. The company does not want to stay at a standstill with their products and just get by with whatever buyers we do sell to. We want to sell every single day so that the small investment that we once out into the Dropshipping business will now amount to a new feat of success.

Often companies do not get to their next earning tier because they are afraid of the automation and they are afraid of dealing with multiple suppliers. Just because it could be the companies first time loading up with new orders and new responsibilities do not mean that this is a mission impossible. This is going to teach the dropshipper more and more what the main focus will be and where the company will want to be going as soon as they put more and more back into their company infrastructure.

Great dropshippers get the job done by dedicating a lot of hard work and time into their projects. If the company legitimately wants to do well in their Dropshipping business they are going to need to have a strong drive and they are going to need to push for their success. Success cannot be achieved off of just a couple of weekly sales every now and then only covering fees to pay service providers. We are going to need to ramp up productions if the company owner is serious and we will begin to finally start making real sales.

Chapter 15: Tips to Make Your Dropshipping Business as Successful as Possible

Focus On the Marketing

Marketing is going to become one of the most important aspects of brand exposure that comes with the company. Marketing is going to motivate a big portion of the sales being made on the company sites and choosing to post about the company at specific times is going to lead a new word for the online world. There are tons of ways to market but some of the main ones that we spoke of in the book are going to be about Facebook ads and Google Adwords.

These two strategies are great when it comes to marketing because they have intricate systems that allow followers to find you in more ways than one. Affiliate advertising will happen when you get great customers that can't help but spread the great word of your company. Indirect marketing is going to be a great vantage point for companies that do not have a whole lot of capital to spend solely on advertising. A company does not need to spend thousands of dollars on their first ad campaigns but there needs to be a general growth formula for all of the products that need showcasing to be sold.

In consideration of marketing, not all products sell themselves and this is going to be a crucial aspect for the dropshipper to touch on when they make their personalized advertisements. Go all out and get professional photos made of the entire product line and write very descriptive product bios to state to the customer the qualities that are in every product.

Do Not Underprice the Products

Know the value of the products and do not low ball the price just for the customer's sake. Try price matching other competing companies with your products to keep a structured value system. If the prices are too low for the consumer there will be assumptions that the shop does not supply quality and that the consumer should beware of what is actually on the product line.

If the company charges too little for their products they are only going to have menial advances like customer reviews to fall back on. This is not going to be good for a startup because no one will know if they are going to trust to buy from the shop or not. Buyers are willing to spend good money on great products so knowing product value is one of the main aspects of running a great shop. Overpricing products in the shop is one thing if anything it will just create a more specific buying crowd but once the company underprices their products it is going to be a minefield for any new customer that comes to the shop. They will not know if they are getting a truly good value or not.

Do not underprice items because the cost of your items or goods are going to need to equal or exceed the amount of money we spend on the services and fees that it takes for us to even list the products on a page and communicate with our warehouse distributors. This is going to be important for shops that have good bargains and are listing them at low rates because these low rates will be great for customers coming in. If these customers do not remain consistent the company is going to end up spending more money every day in the services and fees that it takes to run the whole thing.

Remember to stay conscious of the spending budget and that there is a healthy balance between money incoming and outgoing. All PO's need to be tracked and added up at the end of the month to find what is going in and what is coming out. Money tracking is going to be one of the simplest things to do for the budget and making further movements with bigger investments is going to be a great starting point to the shop's sales.

This is going to be important for bulk shippers that have great deals but also have to remember still not to price each unit so low in price. There are going to source out there that tell you more and more to drop the price and for their reasons only. They do not control your market so likewise when you see competition posting products that are marginally lower than yours or even higher it is best to adjust this given price to a strong median. This price needs to be at the perfect sweet spot and definitely not too low because the business needs to see a return with profits on the items. Stay aware of the market even if it is dropping at an all-time low keep the prices consistent.

Pick a Product That Makes a Good Profit Margin

Pick a product that is going to yield more revenue than it is going to take to get the product sold. This product needs to have brought great assets to the seller so that they can hone in and really define that calling purchasing audience. A good product is going to be a common good or something that most people purchase. These are strong traits for a product because this will ensure that the buying market will never be scarce and there will be plenty of competition to go neck and neck with which isn't always a bad thing.

A product that is on the trending rise and that is being modified through its time is going to be a great seller. These products are going to bring diversity to the shop and it is going to attract customers that are trying to be with the times. These customers will purchase merely upon habit to follow the trend typically and this will make everyone happy. Create a custom product that stands out from the rest and that is easily manufactured so that they can compete with the trending products that are also on the market.

Pick a product that is going to stand on the front lines so that when you also go into making the shop online that you will feel great showcasing this product and that your shop is the source to find it. This product can be colorful or it can have fine stitching or be made out of very good material. The product's best quality is one you are going to capitalize off of and let the rest speak for itself while they check out with it using the shopping cart in the shop.

Find Ways to Bundle Items Together

Bundle items together to make a great deal for oncoming buyers. Have a markdown deal with the purchase of $50 or more and give back to the customers by sending them away with something extra in their shopping bags today. Find ways to offer freebies and discounts for the customers that are very dedicated to the shop. This will give the customer a feeling of both appreciations as well as pride for the shop. If there are special items in stock there can be an event where the customer buys one item and gets another item for free just by acting now and proceeding to the checkout.

These bundle items are going to become popular and you will find that there are going to be dedicated buyers to the shop that are only going to come for the bundled items. And who are we to deny them this love? Because they love the bundle and we gave it to them if it is going well we are also going to ramp this up and offer possible bundle gifts on any redemption of points by dollars spent with the store.

Maybe the customer will have so many points that they save them up and the company will go ahead and send them a birthday gift to enjoy on the shop's dime. This will be a good reward for those that are shopping exclusively at the shop. This is going to be a great reward system for anyone that is frequently visiting the shop. Frequent visitors should be offered extra incentives for being such a dedicated role to the online shop. Give rewards to customers that give good reviews and put stars on product quality for other members of the shop to see.

These bundles can be giving away to customers for product loyalty and it will encourage more individuals to seek these same offers. Sell bundles at a good price and make sure they are equal to other products in the store so that it shares a common spending amount. This spending amount is going to be cost efficient for any of the buyers that come when they weigh different options between purchasing more expensive items or buying the bundle and getting more value and more items for their buck.

Pick the Right Platform

Pick a platform that is going to support your business in every move so that the company and the platform are going towards the same common goals. Pick a platform that has strong communication programs so that you can stay active with the roles that the providers play. Pick a platform that has great support programs so that you can ask specific questions about the systems at hand and if there are any ways to personalize the Dropshipping experience in any way that is possible.

The business is going to need to make custom changes to the sites and all of the supplying partners to truly make the company stand apart from the rest. Communicate openly about any problems or concerns about the platform and make sure they are going to be a secure source that will protect your sensitive data. If they are open about their help to your assets it is going to be easier to calculate the future steps that are made with the business budgets.

Always Provide The Best Customer Service

Always give good customer service whether it is going to be for a new time customer or a customer that has been buying all year. This is going to set the company apart from the rest and will shine on the brand when sales begin to escalate. Package arrival and mail assistance is going to be one of the main factors to stay on top of when it comes to customer satisfaction and if there is confusion towards the business and their shipping routines there will need to be an interactive help guide to walk any customers that are receiving a hard time from purchasing something at the shop.

Verify Your Products Personally Before Selling It

The only way you are going to truly know why your products are selling is if the dropshipping owner touches or feels substantial to the concept of real profit. If the owner specifically tells the realness of the product and to define the quality of their investment they will develop a closer relationship to their supplying partners. If the owner does not physically touch the product also considering it could be an offshore resource the owner can hire a company product manager and this individual will have the responsibilities of product verification.

Verification can stand for a lot of different classifications of product inspections. At times some products are going to need inspecting and even testing to create the one hundred percent guarantee that can put something on the shop shelves. The manager will also be able to track inventory and keep the shipments organized if there are special orders that need more attention than others.

Ordering samples is a great way to get to know a company and its selling ethics. True distributors which can also include wholesalers will sometimes offer samples of their products if the company is willing to purchase in big quantities and the company will understand that the fit will need to be just right for the consumer. Product analysis is necessary to finalize the steps of getting your product out and to the customer.

Feel free to ask for samples of the products that you have not seen yet. Ask the company because they most likely will give you these products to run trials with. For some overseas distributing there is going to typically be extra fees for shipping and handling. There are expensive or altered shipping costs outside of the US so this should be a factor to think about.

Track multiple suppliers' lists and also verify manufacture make or product sources so that there is verification of product authenticity. Every product needs to be authentic and it needs to come from a genuine source that can also be a great partner to begin profits with. There may be a wholesaler in the markets that are able to sell exclusively to partner in the market of their choice.

These are really good relationships to make because there can be major profits generated from the more exclusive these sales become. This can be great for any internal partners that are not integrated within the same companies and this could lead to great profits for quality if the manufactures put all the right pieces together. Some companies manufacture their own products down to the materials and labor.

This is going to be major profits by cutting out all of the middlemen that would be making profits from the other steps that get in the way of normal selling with that of a retail store on the strip. Look at the best products on the market that you are willing to dropship and make sure it is made with quality because it will represent the company.

Conclusion

"Dropshipping E-commerce in 2019" is going to be one of the best reads of the year for anyone who is trying to get into the new age sale of the era. Be prepared to take the skills that were learned in this book and transfer them into the next possible move in life which could be a Dropshipping business. You could be selling tee shirts or collectible seashells across the globe. Maybe your shop already has a company logo and now you want to do some brand marketing. Get aboard the Dropshipping train and enjoy the strategies you are going to learn through service providers like eBay.

Be aware that to run a great shopping website once you successfully take the plunge into creating a website for the company there is going to need to be security for every single piece of information that comes through the seller's website. Take care of these things with certificates that will encrypt your URL and links so that breaches will not try and attack the assets of your company and possibly even crash the whole site is complete and take everything.

Utilize marketing tools like Google Adwords and Facebook ads to gain full exposure to the community that you are engaging with. Remember that the community is going to be an online base so there needs to be consistency if the members begin to become forgetful. Entice them with special offers and make every customer feel great when they come to your shop so that they know they are getting more out of it than any other shop they will trust.

www.ingramcontent.com/pod-product-compliance
Lightning Source LLC
Chambersburg PA
CBHW070229180526
45158CB00001BA/274